Calendars And Clocks

written by: Deion Lee III

First Lulu.com Books Edition, January 2010

 Published In the United States by lulu.com

Library of Congress Cataloging-in-Publication Data

Lee, Deion.

Calendars And Clocks /

Deion Lee

ISBN 978-0-557-25271-8

1. Lee, Deion 2. Poetry
3. Poets-United States-Poetry
4. Ages 18-Senior Citizens
5.Men and Women

Vintage ISBN

978-0-557-25271-8

Manufactured in the United States of America

Dear GOD

Forgive me for my crosses. Deliver me from the demons that come to end my mortal existence. Hide me in Your nest above the savage wolves in the wilderness below. May I bypass the infirmary when I feel weak and decrepit? Send my soul to a room of angels, that's if they will accept it.

I made my road hard to travel, You had it paved out for me; but I walked in the gravel. Was I a prisoner of war in my lack of understanding, or a slave to the Master of Mayhem who extorted me?

What I've done to many, some, and only one; things I once considered to be fun. I realize that the motives and the consequences didn't match. The monotony is murdering me; help me partake in a decent hobby before I self-destruct.

From villainous acts, I have developed bad posture. The look of my face is becoming a placard of what I have been through, and the words I choose to use in dialogue are sounding like sirens to those who want to be closer to me; however, I never meant to alarm them.

Alcohol and tobacco products regularly siphon my saliva, so I'm usually feeling dehydrated, but I'm always delighted to see them come around.

Endemic of Louisiana, which is not the "hot spot" for dating on either side of the gender board, will I commit my body to another woman believing in a vacant promise of forever; only to renege and wish I could ask her for my dick back?

I have witnessed so much suffering, and what nerve of me to have any complaints about my hardships, when it is You who has made the ultimate sacrifice for us all.

Do You mind if I request for a blessing, because I think I am going to need one? Someday a child will require my help, please enable me to feed one!

Lately I've been having disturbing premonitions of my demise, what does it all mean, the images behind my eyes and in the front of my mind? God, are you trying to send subliminal messages to me? I am praying for peace and understanding today.

I am aware that no excuses are permissible for not keeping in touch with You; although if You were to ask me why I have been astray, I must say that it's rather difficult to converse with someone who doesn't talk back to me.

All I want for Christmas annually is the privilege to see another one. Show me the way of righteousness, for it seems I've been walking in a cloud of gas with vision hazed, fading in and out of consciousness.

I'm petitioning for an awakening of my spirit, I know I'm within an earshot of You at all times; so if it is in Your will, please work in my heart to guide my steps into a bright and integral future.

AMEN

If Heaven Was A Mile Away, Would I Pack Up My Bags And Leave This World Behind?

"Nas"

written by: Deion Lee III

The Rain

Maybe he didn't appreciate the things you did to clearly indicate where you wanted to be.

Maybe you had to cry to cleanse away the film of filth that he put in your line of sight.

Maybe it was not your fault, maybe you stumbled upon the devil in human form, and his presence was overwhelming with a charm that kept you warm.

Maybe you leapt before you crept into the mind of a deceiver, maybe he made you a believer, to make you feel that when he left, you would see yourself as an underachiever.

Maybe you've been naive, namely bland in your discretion, or looked to an individual to provide your heart with protection.

Overcast

Maybe the kiss he gave made you feel like a child tasting candy for the first time, and

maybe loving him was like skydiving but forgetting the fear of heights.

Maybe he is miserable now though he proceeds with the facade of happiness and laughter.

Maybe his indecision and cursed pride will not allow him to admit his fallacies to evade the burden of shame.

Maybe when you closed the door another opened and in front of it I stood.

Maybe the fear of me eventually resembling the demon you despise tells you not to come close, but I think you should.

Light Drizzle

Maybe the moment you close your eyes you dream before you fall asleep. Maybe I don't know what I'm talking about, it's said that talk is cheap.

Maybe you've been sabotaged into unmerciful language; I bear the same

burdens so how else could I explain it. Maybe I sound contemptuous because this is a contingency; maybe we should have kept it, yeah our precious virginity.

Maybe I'm your hero, from your bad days I will save you. Maybe I'm the villain and my mission is to enslave you.

Maybe I'll be good to you, on my best behavior, like gum that's chewed for a while: (eventually I'll lose all my flavor). Maybe you will spit me out or add another piece to me, either way I must say that I hope that's not how you do me*

Maybe I'm confused, thinking too hard in the process. Maybe I don't understand that what you can't rush is progress.

Heavy Rain

Maybe you went left, assuming it was the right way, felt like you had to stay with him regardless of what people might say.

Maybe the spot that you are in was premeditated; pessimism was your

persecutions aren't you glad that you made it?

Maybe others could see it coming, like meteorologists forecast, or maybe you were part karma, even if it wasn't your past.

Maybe you're drowning in heartache, as I stand on your shoulders, it's the American Way: (Everyone's Trying To Get Over).

Maybe my words have no value and I'm rambling onward, with the rest of the world that I have set out to conquer~

The Flood

"After all is washed away, and no structure seems to remain, we pick up the fragments and rebuild our foundations. The rain will come again and again, so I suggest we make preparations. "

written by: Deion Lee III

Imagine

We were in another place where nothing existed except for the two of us. Where would that place be?

If I was forewarned that my time would be limited to 24 hours to live, would I be able to reach you fast enough to weep and rejoice in your company.

If your favorite song was playing at the dance and the only person you wanted to groove with was absent.

Think of the moments that I've spent vividly illustrating what I meant when I spoke of LOVE.

Did it conquer all your fears evaporating all your tears, sublimate the previous years into newfound bundles of cheer.

If I was washed away at sea, no boat

or plane to rescue me, would you sail the course from time to time to view my reflection in the water shine.

What mayhem would ensue if anyone attempted to bring harm to you? My understanding would vanish and rage becomes the only rationality for my act of revenge.

Selling a multi-platinum record would be nice, but so much more delightful would be witnessing one person happily sing a song I exclusively dedicated to you.

If I had a shirt with your name on it after the words I love, and I wore it in one of the largest arenas in the world with permission to be spotlighted for 60 seconds for the masses and media to capture, all I could say is...

Imagine

written by: Deion Lee III

Phantasmagoria

I'm pharisaical at times, but who isn't? I'm an advocate of peace; however under the right or wrong conditions I could commit assault or murder.

This would thrust me over the threshold of what I stand for, into a temporary residence of my own oppositions.

So I have a general idea of who I am, but the truth is: I don't and probably will not ever know myself.

Bewilderment...

On a secular search for higher learning, I rummage through aggravated streets.

Litter lies where the grass and the concrete meet.
The bright sunshine and pillow-like clouds are the only visible items to mitigate my dilapidated surroundings.

How much misery can one set of eyes intercept before the will to indefinitely sleep presides?

Our dignitaries are acting as degenerates in secrecy as well as without shame. I support religion.

If whosoever it is you believe that has control over your life is responsible for helping you to live righteously, then I see no cause to protest, whether it be GOD or a statue that you choose to worship.

Miseducation...

Television evangelists, men of GOD mind you, are performing miracles every Sunday in the midst of the congregation behind them and watched by a vast audience of home viewers as well.

An elderly person approaches him with the assistance of a wheelchair exclaiming his or her ailment of not being able to walk amongst other disabilities and impairments.

The evangelist chants a prayer and sprinkles a lil' water over the patrons head.

Next, within an instant the elderly one springs from the wheelchair as if he or she had been using a trampoline and proceeds to dance vigorously with joy, synonymous to reenacting an epileptic seizure.

Well, is that not hypocrisy in its finest suit? Does this not send a mixed signal to our children; do we want them to think that mankind possesses the same level of power as GOD?

What gives any of us mortals the right to deny that there is only one true healer?

We demand honesty from the youth when we want to know if they are sexually active or recreationally using drugs, and most adults haven't the

slightest clue that the primary reason for the mass rebellion in their offspring is warranted from their failure to be brutally honest with them.

Hence, who do your children admire now, what people serve as their role models today?

(The athletes, entertainers, gangsters, and others of the sort.)

FEAR...

Not much moves me in the spirals of darkness to make me believe that there is something I should need protection from.

Recognizing the danger but not responding with anger, the evening news is depressing, our future is so uncertain, but I refuse to seek refuge in my home and watch the world through my curtains.

I ask the Lord for mercy, but could not ask that from a man, I'd laugh if confronted by one with a gun in his hand.

You may say that's foolish, but fear doesn't live, its value is not enough for anyone to want to give.

Nightmares from R.E.M. sleep can rattle my nerves, yet once I have awakened I guess the images were learning curves.

Oddly so, I reckon this is my method of philanthropy, living and dying within the realms of...

Phantasmagoria

written by: Deion Lee III

Inquiry And Interest

Yeah I did it, not just to say that I did it, but I'm committed. Allow me to ask you what is better than the best?

And if you know of something that is, you've been advised to clench it expeditiously. Nothing is literally endless except maybe the universe and time itself.

Although, I don't believe me saying our love range is interminable would be an exaggeration. Do you?

I'm imagining myself gloating about the way your jawbone tickles my lips, when I kiss you on the face and place my hands aside your hips, and what have you...

I know this is off the subject text; but neccessary to say, that no one can make life harder for me than I have made it for myself already.

I am willing to bet all I have; which isn't enough to afford losing, that any rational person would agree with me, putting it in perspective with themselves that is.

There is no such thing as instant

gratification. And don't you know that there is a process to every course of action to be taken for anything to be achieved?

Regardless of how hard it may be for you to fathom, because of you *I BELIEVE*. Could I trust you to help me improvise and devise plans to reach my dreams whether or not those dreams are matching or in any way in conjuction with what you want to fulfill?

This is what *I NEED* to know. When I make a dream come true, several more for multitudes materialize along with that. Your concerns and opinions of what I do is more than enough.

This man makes the money to ameliorate the family tree, so money doesn't make the man; but I'm accepting donations like the United Negro College Fund amongst other accredited charities. (Laughter Is Appropriate Here)

I'm joking, yet simultaneously serious so pardon my effrontery. One may ask, "How can you joke and also be serious?" My answer to that would be, "All I have left is my sense of humor and honesty."

Subserviently, I would like to build a colony of people who progress and thrive with you. From our children, to their children, and further along to the ones we will not have the chance to see grow. Because we all have our time to, "GO."

Consult with those who know me best to corroborate my testimony. Let's go to recess before further counsel, hold your inquiries and interests until we continue, this meeting is adjourned...

written by: Deion Lee III

Unforgettable

Does it bother you that the thought of me fades in and out of your mind like fireflies under the moonlight? The moment my eyes could no longer see your car leaving my street, it was then I realized that I was missing you.

To know someone has a vast array of ambient challenges and rather tedious dreams lying ahead of them; hence, regardless of the ambivalence you feel, you find the strength and capacity to say that being around for it all has been a blessing.

Furthermore, that you will have the time and patience to hold on when it seems like the braids of thread in your conjoint rope is starting to splinter.
(Remembering...) She said to me, "I've almost climbed this Rocky Mountain to its peak, please don't let me fall now!"
If an opinion can't be formed through reasoning and information, should one rely on what is implied? I said to her, "My

intentions are not to let you down, but to lift you higher."
I look around and see a young happy couple and smile briefly, then hang my head low in comparison of where I stand today. Thinking about what I <u>had</u> as well as what she <u>lost</u>.
When you ask who loves me now, I'm taciturn wanting to say, "No one, but soon enough more than I can count will love me artificially and genuinely."
Wondering why fo' do ya' make such an inquiry, as if there was some sort of pun in the content of the question, I pause...

Leaving impressions in your panties, although my hands were in my pockets, you were standing in an awry position as if to hide the moisture accumulating in and around your slip-n-slide area. Did you take a trip down memory lane by chance?
Hmmm... People fall in and out of love daily, I wonder why that is; possibly it is the way we approach the idea of longevity unknowingly producing its brevity. Reminiscing of escapades we had, I am glad. And the moments I once thought to be unbearable in reality aren't so bad.
She talked about forever, but she changed

her mind, or perhaps a change of heart? Moreover, was either even involved from the start? Something to think about right, when in reference to life?
Another page in a new chapter, reading from the same book, the setting is still morose, the plot thickening by the second, closer to the end yet dubious to look onward, and leery of how I may feel once I finish.
After a downpour of rain one Sunday afternoon, she solemnly said to me, "I looked into a puddle of water, collected an image of your smile, and felt remorsefully vile."

Per Diem, she says that men shoot wild game with her in their crosshairs, and they miss the intended target with amateurish aim.
We would laugh when humor was absent and love when malicious vibes arose, we would cry when strength was more appropriate to have, and kiss them away from each other's faces. Priceless!

She also said to me, "There are times I pout, knowing I have to do without an expert love engineer. All is black and all is white, life is plain within my sight, sometimes I might try to redecorate rooms in my house to suppress the prominent portraits I've seen of you on furniture. With no luck in that, I will draw a pretty picture of something with fluorescent flavor to liven-up my existence minus you."

Tension and relaxation interchange, and we remember in a hallucinogenic sense of thought from whatever we choose to induce it, if not naturally. History has been created and now, from our foreheads to the back of our minds, we are always...

UNFORGETTABLE

written by: Deion Lee III

Still I believe, that true love will always find its' home.

The Jukebox

He is "The Jukebox" so as long as you pay, he shall continue to play.

He serenades a lady under the beautiful notes of an unusual love stream giving permission to float.

R&B

He is a crooner, one who can make you climax sooner, compelling a damsel in distress to remove her dress, and circle her hips slow, like a dance of calypso.

Touching erogenous zones unknown, surpassing inflation of a mind to one fully BLOWN. Every woman wants to feel pompous and grand, like the leader of a world renowned marching band.

He is the creator of butterflies in the pit of a stomach, and although life has a way of making you believe that you have lost, his lyrics and melodies have priceless treasures you gain from it.

The good feeling you keep in memory of what he said to reach millions; however, the potency of the product gives you the right to claim it as your very own ode to royal treatment.

SOUL

Excavation of what lies beneath your exterior and bringing it to surface for the world abroad to witness. When trial, tribulation, and the seemingly harshest adversity have landed on your lawn, he identifies with it and shares the burden.

Never leaving your side to tend to other matters as long as the record plays; he is resilient, absolutely fuckin' brilliant for being able to move the immaterial essence of an individual life, and in choice cases even save a life.

Who could make one laugh when there is nothing amusing? Or cry because you have been graced with an inkling of triumphant hope when the resonance of failure was the only song you ever sang?

In a deep chord of sincerity and sympathy, one is able to embrace his hand without its tangency available; the substance is most closely associated with an unconfirmed healing ritual.

Alternative Rock

Would you believe it if you heard it? You may have thought he was another race if you never saw his face, he's the rock and the roll, 27 years old, loves his guitar more than any human being except his mother and sister.

With an acoustic in his company he could draw a crowd from the sidewalk. Not too heavy to dull the senses, but just light enough to massage your skull. Taking the migraines away replacing them with a soothing balance of thought, the album you wish you would have bought.

Guessing and checking the pop and country grooves, he's a southern soldier fighting to bring the old days in accord with the current ones. For the rural areas he represents its inhabitants, down to Earth and never going above anyone's' head in them.

Over-extroverted in his stylistics, a gatherer of opinion and controversy, and scenic in foresight to deliver an enlarged image to the commonly simple ideas most of us envision.

HIP-HOP

Something like the chain and ball that knocked down the Berlin Wall, strong enough to have been responsible for the fall of the Roman Empire, the martyr of independence and struggle.

He paints many pictures of all colors, shapes, and sizes. The evidence of what a child can become with creativity and a crayon. That's if you don't stick one in your ear, He did and it hurt when the doctors removed it. (Laughing My Ass Off)!

Many children's' role model, forever influential to be cherished by the world. He spends more time imagining than realizing, it's the dreamer in a vivid storyteller. An advocate of the slums first, then empathetic to others afterwards.

He has fun working with the less fortunate, meanwhile keeping his ego at an all-time high as the master of ceremonies.

"THE JUKEBOX" is here to stay, so when he dies, press play and bring him back to life...

Coming soon to a neighborhood and television set near you!

written by: Deion Lee III

You're Nobody Till Somebody Kills You

What? Nigga Bring It!!!
You don't have to look very far or with any effort to find me, I am not hiding!
Your idle threats are silly and shameful, you aren't using violence, but your objective is to project strength to intimidate your opposition.

Well HA HA, the jokes on you dumbass, I am neither rattled nor in any way scared of your antics.

Little do you know; I don't even have to lift a finger on either hand to cease your existence.
I know at least 5 people who wouldn't give it any thought to blow your house off the foundation if I were to advise them of the games you are playing with The Jukebox.
Ask yourself, do you really want to have to relocate your immediate family to another city or state because of some shit you started with a quiet, peace advocate?
Don't get it twisted like pretzels and licorice sticks, I'm skinny but dangerous!

In fact, you may want to go and purchase a lifetime supply of adult diapers, because at the rate you are going, I will most likely have to put you in a

dependent situation.
I don't mind making you relive your infantile stages of life, I will have you shitting all over yourself, NO QUESTION!
Take it all in and under careful consideration before you run up on me. I'm not an irrational counter-attack.

I mastermind all angles of destruction. If I'm cornered, you will be the victim of a heinous crime, unaware that the plot was from me.

So imagine this, checking the perimeter outside the entrance door to your home before you exit.

Envision a man dressed in black wearing a SCREAM mask greeting you with a baseball bat to your throat, stifling your regular respiratory pattern, and then pressing a chloroform rag over your face until you lose consciousness.
Then dragging you into a vehicle, driven to an undisclosed wooded area, laid out on the ground, and stripped of your clothing to be saturated with a few gallons of bleach.

By the time you regain consciousness, your skin will be hideously corroded by the potency of the chlorine, fucked up and alone if not dead.
Grotesque right?
So if you want to be famous or earn stripes

amongst your peers, I suggest you pursue a career
in the entertainment industry instead of making
the headlines in the evening news.

For example of course, the consequences and
repercussions can and more than likely will be
much worse in every detail.

Don't think twice; think several times before you
cross these unventured borders.

Ya feel me?
I reminisce on dead friends too...
Because YOU'RE NOBODY TIL SOMEBODY
KILLS YOU!

written by: Deion Lee III

Sugarpuffinpoohbear

Did you know that I really love you? And I just want to thank you now for all the joy you bring, furthermore the fulsome exhilaration and wonders that you will present later.

My eyes may be a little glossy from the effects of my habits, but I C U, do you see me? I'm staring at ya.

My ears take in a lot, but there will always be room for you to be heard in them. I feel like I'm in reverie when I think about you. The awkward part is when I become distracted and snap out of it. I would gladly walk you home, but you are already here baby, living within the walls of my spirit.

I got a glimpse of what spending everyday of the rest of my life with you would be like. I know you see me standing over here in the darkness, flash me and shine your light this way.

Let me specify, this is the resurgence of The Rhyme Scholar. In my mind it has occurred to me that you are not only *something*, but also ***everything*** *pertinent in my days and nights.*

You have brought me back to my essence in its entirety. I will be certain to harbor and cherish your love infinitely, if it is your desire for me to do so.

You are like a meal I crave frequently, and so easy to digest. I have found it imperative that we become and remain much more than friends. I don't even think we have actually begun, and I can't fathom the juncture of when it will end.

I wonder if you saw me

coming, I thought my intentions were so obvious? Initially, I just wanted you to get an idea of who I am, and then leave it at your discretion whether or not to help me learn about you.

I am amazed, fact is that I feel like I've known you since my childhood, our hearts are synchronized, we move parallel in thought pattern, and from the very instant you embraced me as a man; your grip hasn't loosened, it tightens as we proceed.

Right now, I'd like you to close your eyes, imagine and fantasize about what you would like to do to me, with me, and for me. Vice versa, feign those things which you would like me to do to you, with you, and for you.

Now open your eyes and hear me when I say...

It Will Be Much More Than That!

MY SUGARPUFFINPOOHBE AR

written by: Deion Lee III

Pulse

This is the pique of a man. Fact not fiction, heartbreak never breaks evenly. One side is pulverized so to speak, and the other is relieved in some margin.

Without suffrage on the situation, your pulse will modify itself. For informative purposes, when you are me: Everything you do will be examined with elaborate energy. And all that I speak of will be regarded with sincerity and I will be expected to serve exponentially as one who stands behind every syllable in each word that leaves my mouth.

On a date with destiny, she gives me a terminal condition of the heart. I could die like cast metal, from the symmetry of her sympathy. More than less, the affection is as tacit as an infants' love for his or her primary caregiver.

When one has been given a reason to feel special, that is grounds for reciprocating the love without a vertebral column. Oh, what a quandary! If I take her hand will she crush mine within her palm, or tenderly caress it all over and keep me calm. She provides an uncanny sense of hope for me to grasp and challenges my mind as I am the student who is ready to learn the lessons she is overqualified to teach me. However, she can reach me.

What if I perform poorly on my exams and I fail to meet the requirements to graduate to Higher Learning? The prior student cheated his way into obtaining a certificate Doctorate degree in Love Adequacy.

He's in the process of losing his credentials so much faster than he earned them. So of course, she may be predisposed to thinking that I'm "up to something",

and she will make my criteria
substantially harder to complete.

Being married is similar to employment
from what my eyes can see; and although
I've yet to take a stroll down that aisle,
I've been around for a while. Long enough
to know that if you don't perform
satisfactorily on this particular
assignment, chances are that you will get
FIRED, and in this love recession,
EVERYBODY needs a job!

Are you feeling a change in the regular
throbbing of your arteries caused by
contractions of the heart? Feeling faint
from the punitive damages you are
responsible for? If so, this would be a
perfect time to attempt reconciliation,
heed the warning or you will be left for
the caring and charismatic without a...

Pulse

This literary piece was intentionally

designed to scare some sense into those who take their loved ones for granted!

Think About It.

written by: Deion Lee III

Chardonnay Charade

I'm not complaining, it's sustaining me, you should know this modifies my sedentary lifestyle. Swallowing the remedy for any discomfort when I taste you; run from me and I'll chase you.

The consummate homemaker, a martyr, and resplendent in your gait. I find your distinctive attitude alluring, I lionize your sex, and I savor the moments in which you are fond of me.

I've escaped domestication, hence I

am running wild. Accolades bestowed unto you because I do appreciate your candor. I'm mired by your majesty; the thought of us is so quixotic, but I'm considering all possibilities and not convinced that this liquid love affair will incapacitate me in any way.

With each dose I take of you, I rise higher above sea level. If only I had the answer to this question: How is it possible that your substance quells my fear of crashing?

My equanimity has unquestionably vanished with celerity. Your lenses recorded it instantly. How did that cognizance draw you? Did you dance internally, perhaps it felt as though your heart skipped a beat?

You are sublime, inspiration, and
somehow our relationship is
symbiotic enough to encourage us
to elope. Although my time with
you may be a sojourn, meanwhile; I
will be loitering along your
novelties in hope of an odyssey.

It's ironic how, sporadically when I
look at you my vision is a haze from
the formation of tears in my eyes
and anything beyond the hair that
falls over your ears is vaguely
noticed; the only emotion I claim is
an iridescent happiness.

Help me understand the lucid
dream in my mind, I move at a

languid pace, this is not a race, I respect your space, see an empty frame, and what appears next is your face. Almost unwilling to relinquish your affections, so don't speak.

I will guess the next action in sequence of us. With valor I am standing on this battlefield, and this is my affidavit of insurance to consume you until the very last drop: win, lose, or draw.

My Ever So Sweet Chardonnay Charade

written by: Deion Lee III

SCREAM

If I've neglected your cries and concerns, I am truly apologetic knowing that my ***screams*** drowned out the voices I needed to hear.

Damn! I don't know when to go to sleep or when to wake up; my schedule is ever-changing. My mind is filled beyond capacity with images, thoughts, and emotions. So before I damage or destroy the infrastructure, allow me to lend some of these things to you.

I recently learned that my mother has a growth of some sort in her head, which is non-threatening as of now; however, it is only a matter of time before surgery must ensue, amongst other disturbing factors that I can't possibly speak of or else I would automatically crack into pieces.

Not eavesdropping, but accidentally

I overheard something I don't believe I was supposed to that her husband was discussing with someone; and I can't even tell my mother or any other relative of mine.

What I want to say may be so catastrophic that mentioning anything would be more detrimental than beneficial. She's been through enough.
These days fly by so rapidly, like the jets from the nearby air-force base. Where the fuck did time go? A usual ray of sunshine I am, but I feel more like I'm the victim of horror in a film.

Who is the author of the story of my life? Oh yeah! **GOD**. How could I forget the paper cuts from flipping the pages of **The Good Book**? I'm slipping.

I met this particular one who should have a national monument built in resemblance of her image with a caption beneath her mold outlining and defining her attributes and characteristics; more importantly what a real good example of a woman is and should be.

Decisions, decisions... Do I cut my hair today or let my nappy roots continue outward? I told Bobby not to lose sight of the bigger picture because so much more is meant for us to achieve. Incarceration made us both impatient, but we are still waiting in a sense.

Do I expose a person in a position of authority to my ignorance in order to orchestrate a change in the way I am being treated on my job? I don't think my superior is fully aware that I am a hair away from getting a lawsuit and/or being charged with aggravated battery.

People don't value the things that we all should. Try to remember that someone has it rougher than your own mind can imagine, and that is reality at its finest. Even when it seems we have lost, we actually made it!

I'd like to dance with someone sometimes when I show at a club, but every time I take a woman by the hand in there, she acts as if she's fucking me on the dance floor. It feels more raunchy than romantic, not saying I don't like it, but ya know decency is preferred every now and then.

Perhaps you should lie to me more often; the truth does puncture me soul very badly. I saw that same old lady who hasn't changed clothes in years foraging through a garbage heap for something to eat. I offered to bring her a hot meal, but she told me no. Confused and crying I turned away.

Numbers and letters we communicate to make this world better or worse, technology may be our enemy as well as a friend. In silence I pray because if **GOD** ever speaks to me, I want to be certain that **His** message is clear.

Some random female looks at me as if I am to marvel and fancy her incandescent features, but I don't seem to care if she's fine and big-breasted. My attention is arrested by personality alone, which she lacks so I don't ring her phone.

Peace on Earth sure is when you rest beneath its surface. I see dead people; I do look in the mirror everyday ya know. I'm so alive!

Being human sucks in a major way sometimes, if there are alien life forms present on other planets, I may be able to get adjusted quite well to abduction; so if the Martians can tune in on this frequency, read and comprehend this, I'm game for an outer space adventure.

Pardon me but, all of what I've just said actually does make me want to

SCREAM

Male Quote For The Day:

"Bite Your Tongue Or Let Your Nutz Hang!"

I'm positive that I will need to share more with you as time rolls on, thanks a mega load for listening!

And The Jukebox Plays On And On...

written by: Deion Lee III

January Embers

The woman I happen to love is married to another man. Before you cast a stone or judge me, take a moment to understand.

Usually, I would not entertain such thoughts of having what belongs to someone else. What began as a friendship became more of a shoulder to lean on. And now, even though we know lines are being crossed, in our delirious comfort and unyielding happiness nothing seems wrong.

I am technically single; however, I am not, she lives within me and regulates the way I function like the components of my heart. When I see this woman, I am anxious to watch the smile break across her face.

On several occasions, I have found it difficult to relinquish the smile I present to her in return as if my jaws were frozen. I feel

jealously possessive with the hope
that one day she will choose me,
but ironically I somehow sense
that I have been chosen already.

Too many words have rolled off
my tongue and into a warm,
acceptable form of supportive
companionship. The moment I
open my eyes from unretained
dreams, I wonder if she is feeling
well, anticipating my phone to
ring, and throughout the
remainder of the day this
incorporates love as the theme.

And before the black shade fades

over my eyes of glaze, she is an addition to my time to pray, a contributory cause of why I walk this way.

Savoring our sugary, sweet memories, assessing how much they mean to me, and what I should do to provide her with the reassurance that her affections towards me are not illustrated in vain; she is the last person I think about, before oblivion sets in my brain.

I'm selfish, vulnerable, sensitive, and also rather cocky to a fault.

I'd blame her if I wasn't aware that it's my fault.

Beyond coincidences such as us being born in the same hospital almost a thousand miles away from the metroplex we met in and currently live; our minds are simultaneously open twenty-four hours each day, extracting all that life has to offer on a quest to expand our horizons into virtually unbelievable sights, this is a profound rarity which leaves me to assume we were meant to belong together.

She inspires me while I'm in pursuit of a career in my expertise and she loves like tomorrow will not appear. I say it's shameful that the man she calls a husband fails to honor and appreciate the virtue of a queen. Worse, knowing when the hour of her departure from him comes, remorse he will not feel, but find it necessary to decimate her character amongst those who will listen.

I've always thought that love only goes so far, in instances where unity is not an option if the other side is withdrawing; because love will meet you halfway or somewhere in the middle, no one deserves having to chase their partner or hypothesize information and intent as if the relationship was a riddle.

It may take time to manifest the situation we want and in the meantime she thinks I may be better suited in other arms, guilt is a ghostly emotion who tends to follow and haunt.

Be that it may, I don't feel as if I am missing out on anything; but rather preserving endless love for my soulmate. The odds are fifty/fifty; however, my feet are firmly planted and my weight isn't shifty.

A package deal with a leaky trail of bitterness from the ex-factor will be what I have to look forward to for the rest of my life. I don't stress about it, keeping in mind that I will be seen years later as a heroic man, eventually respected for saving three lives.

I see the end of the road telescopicly, hell is raising children, a woman has been scorned and almost convinced to settle for what she is best without.

Flames are so high the heat intensity makes anyone who dares to come close reverse, seemingly cursed; and behold... The caped crusader swoops down to rescue the trio, with loves' angel on his back and a child prodigy on each of his shoulders, flying up, far away, and out of January Embers.

written by: Deion Lee III

Therapeutic Sex II

Furthermore, I use my tongue to press against her vaginal walls, and wiggle it from side to side in conjunction with sucking her clitoris between my teeth.

No masquerade, she sees me, we call it Joy Division when her thighs fold outward easily. If she wasn't so meretricious I may have been able to condense my adrenaline, but I know now that will not be possible.

Based on personal merit, she makes me want to share it; I will reward her with my love in its physical form. My face is in a space of mint condition, though I've ran down this avenue before ***I WANT SUM MORE...***

She is squirming like there is some sort of discomfort, but she's begging me not to stop. While I'm dining inside of her my hands grip and tenderize supple breasts, maneuvering around her stomach down to her feet. She rubs my head as if it were a lamp that would grant wishes.

It's amazing how the moans of sheer pleasure can excite a man, invite a man, and take over him. I'm wrapped up like a burrito.

Abruptly stopping to push my love inside, we merge, we mesh, and now we are connected. Turning her body temperature up like the dial on a stove, we may just cook up ourselves a baby if I deposit my load.

Still inside of her, I picked her up and she straddled me all the way to the bed, where I disengaged and threw her down. She bounced right back up to her knees trying to suck out my sperm, now my head feels even more relaxed like a perm.

Next, she screams, "Fuck me." So I bend her over, she puts her hands on the edge of the bed; I kick her feet out a little because I like the image spread. I pull on her hair and pound deep inside, my free hand spanks her ass, then words like: harder, faster, ooh, and yes are being said.

I told her to climb on top of me. She did in a hurry, crashing into me with brisk kisses, slapping some good pussy up and down on me in what seemed like a flurry. I tried to keep a grip on her ass, but my fingers were sliding in the juice, and I'm thinking to myself, “Now this is how you seduce."

Breasts in my mouth, I feel an eruption coming on and want to slow down, but it's too intense and she knows it. She says, "Cum for me daddy I know you're about to blow it. I've had multiple orgasms, I lost count after three. Baby you have no idea what you do to me!"

I felt my body tense up and ejaculated so much, I fell asleep inside of her and by the time we woke up, I saw some dripping out of her when we went to wash up.

This is a memoir of a moment in life that everyone should experience, good luck and happy hunting for...

<u>Therapeutic Sex II</u>

written by: Deion Lee III

Nobody Understands Me

"Well, Hello Miss! My first name is Lee, the middle is Martell Deion Anthony, and my last name is also Lee. Odd right? I am the III, named after my father who I have not any recollection of; which doesn't make me feel low, in fact it make me grow just to know that he never cared whether I was dead or alive."

"You could say I realized at an early age that this world is damned and unforgiving, only the strong will survive. So what's your poison? What would those who know you best consider to be utterly atrocious about you, that's if they would be *friendly* enough to tell you?"

"What's your angle? What is it that you want, need, expect, or demand from me as a person initially, not in reference to friendship or love, but the basics, sugar let's face it? You're anxious to figure out what makes my clock tick; and the first impression, whether better or worse is created to stick."

"Notice my eyes are parallel with yours, maybe I'll check out your breasts later. My forwardness is purposely perforated with purpose; see that I am scratching your surface to peel away the layers. Don't take offense to or shy away from me, I've been known to get under skin like nerves."

"Your admission of wanting to have sex on the first date would prompt me to respect you more. It takes a great deal of courage to embrace such a connection that you refuse to ignore it. This is neither an attempt to score nor a test to determine if you are a whore, it's an innovative theory you've never heard before, a unique mind for you to explore."

"I found out that using your head may save your ass, and a cunning conversation with a woman could = to cash. Shhh! Now, before you lean too far into your own understanding, that does not constitute a contrivance for pimping or prostitution in my case. I have a sedulous mind containing the sagacity of a geriatric man. Just thinking aloud."

"So lose the odious gape, before a fly lands in your mouth, and please pick this conversation up if you feel that it's going south. Three things we have in common are that we have become accustomed to handling and managing liaisons, lechery, and lies. Time and tangents have made us wise."

"I wish I wasn't so complex at times, but I suppose it's for the best somehow; often my body sends signals to my brain that rest is needed, however my mind will not leave me alone, the result is insomnia."

"What is the one thing that you feel as though you can't live without? Honestly, I don't know anyone who can say and mean that if the choice of abundant riches or genuine love was offered to them, that they would select love without hesitation, except for me of course."

"Have you ever touched a heart as well as broken one in the same sentence? I am ashamed to say I did it, but not to admit it on several occasions, and still today I hold repentance. The door is open to my heart; would you like to make an entrance?"

"That's rhetorical I know, but who else would address themselves as such, not many correct? I reflect and recollect that few have faith, most want proof. Not me though, I don't feel like I'm in any position to request a report of your doings and your whereabouts."

"It may seem as if I lack care and concern in ways that I will deal with you, I'm far from a private eye or one who makes an effort to pry. I am always attentive, but never worrisome. Instead of having my nose in your business, I'd rather keep it on my face where it belongs."

"I'm flabbergasted and somewhat envious of people who devote any portion of their day into investigating the behavior of their significant other when they aren't around."

"I mainly rationalize it as a waste of time trying to find fault in someone you want to be closer to, that would seem to create more of a wedge than a link, and my daily itinerary doesn't have room for such preposterous activity. Lucky me!"

"Are we in sync with each other yet, or am I moving further out of your reach? This is very taboo for me to discuss with you, but I'm sure you've recognized that I don't fit into the ordinary category."

"This is only a synopsis of much more to come if you are willing and able to stay a while. I confess I can be a bit of a sycophant because I've been evaluated and regarded by a large number of women who say that I'm suave, debonair, urbane, polished, sophisticated, and etcetera..."

"But I'm not vain, this world couldn't possibly revolve around me; there isn't even half of a chance for anything remotely close to that happening."

If you feel as though I *owe* you an explanation for why I have made these statements, a credit card has been swiped down the crevice of your ass, just put it on my tab because...

Nobody Understands Me

Written by: Deion Lee III

Broken Leg

My mother once told me, "You may have been hurt, but you will also heal. At least now you can say that you know how it feels."

Intangible fields and the desires they yield.
Reach for the sky and all that can be seen with
an eye.
How far did I go and was anything discovered
that I did not already know?

Well it seems as though I have been to hell and
back for a second time; however, I am not

clear. Perhaps I earned my injury on one of
life's treadmills, running in place with nowhere
to go.

I discovered that neither clothes nor the
gangster persona I embody can cover me; my
heart is naked as a newborn out of the womb.
And, regardless of what I may have thought,
my time has been bought.

When running is no longer an option, it is even
harder to walk away, and please is not enough
to make someone stay.
Sucker for love once again, how did she bring

me to my knees? For what seemed like years,

but has actually been less, I was carried like

loose leaves in the breeze.

I censure her for my handicap; which made

luxury the only lap I could feel comfortable in.

Although the handshakes and hugs from false

friends and unbelievable support from gullible

fans have kept me mobile, I somehow feel

ashamed, very far from being noble.

If a smile defines happiness then I have

mislead many of you, for I am so blue.

Furthermore, small is my talk, which is also

cheaper than me offering to buy a woman a drink who I noticed already had one.

I'm ready to throw away my crutches and stand on my own; even if that means I live on screens and in my palace I dwell alone. I have never looked at life in a light so dim, so why would I ask you to get in a boat with me if I know you cannot swim.

Should the vessel overturn, my cast will anchor me to the ocean floor, and we will drown in a "Sea Of Love." As tragic as it may sound, I've always preferred to die with her opposed to dying without her.

Oh, but she can break me down with her anger, yes it chills me to the bone! However, she puts each shattered piece of me together again with the simplest of phrases in monotone.

Such as: "I need you, I miss you, and I love you."

Although these things are seldom said, her words are like aspirin to the ache in my body and in my head. Lately, I've been fuckin' up, with worries and overwhelming stress, it's not an excuse; but, I confess that I haven't been at my best.

Amanda is LOVE, and if I live for LOVE, which I do, this means I live for her too. I remember the day she listened to my heartbeat as we lay in bed. Amanda you will probably never know how much that meant to me and the fact that you said you enjoyed the moment means even more.

Amanda, I ask that you bear with me in my crippled state through the worst of times, which seem to be ongoing. I believe you know more about me than what you do not know about me, and likewise, the feeling is mutual on my behalf.

We both have grown prone to asking one another about the mysteries within, seeking to find comfort in our replies. Meanwhile, we should just be content with the information readily accessible to us.

Forgive me for those times I opened my mouth to criticize, because all I see is how GREAT you are when I look into your eyes. All of what has happened has made me realize how much of a fool I have been. Without you, Dear Amanda, I lose more than I could ever win in this lifetime.

This world is so parasitic, do not let it reduce me to nothing and wither away from your memory. I have no pride, nothing to hide, and I want you to someday take the weight of my last name and be my bride.

And forget the satchel; all I want for Christmas annually is YOU! I have been moving along in our relationship slowly and impaired as if my leg were broken; however, I am healing at a miraculous rate of speed.

Amanda, I love you and I want everyone to know it, and due to my acknowledgement that I have not loved you in proper shape; I feel like it is only right to talk about my **BROKEN LEG**.

But I am still standing for you Amanda; will you continue to stand with me?

Written by: Deion Lee III

Alcoholics Anonymous

Lower the blinds over my mind
With a bottle of cheap wine,
Becoming careless to soon become carefree
For it seems like the place to be.

With no headlights on,
Traveling down such a dark road,
How am I to find my way?

Bearing more than my own load,
How heavy my burden, a scale could not
weigh.

Everyone agrees that some help would be
useful to me,
And though it may be true, I don't want it.

When I'm sober I feel older and find more to
be wrong,

Perhaps I drink to find others to be more
interesting
And add resonance to my song.

Disorder or not, every day I question myself
As to whether I'm leaning towards being vain
Or simply on the borderline of being insane.

Extra I am indeed, but nowhere close to
ordinary.

Rather than criticize my outlandish behaviors
And uncommon humor extent,
Would it not be diplomatic of a woman to
think of me
In this sense..

As more to marry, or perhaps a colorful purse
to carry?

I grew up with a pimp state of mind,

Seems like I'm losing my edge.

I'm falling in love now, yes.
Awkward balance of my affections threw me
over the ledge.

Suicide romance, either die in her arms from
loving her so long
Or die from the fatigue of chasing her shadow
If she chooses to move along.

If so, I did it to myself.
I've heard it said that love is to die for,
Then what is the relevance of health?

I smoke and wonder,
And in my heart I feel a thunder
Like a seismic wave, pillage and plunder.

Taking my breath away, knowing that this

might be the day,
That I rest as I've never rested, my soul can be arrested.

I will lay down my weapons, settle my rage,
And submit to my persecution, no matter my age.

Hung in a hall of shame, is where my picture may be,
Versus the fame I feel deserving of, where will they lay me?

Trouble is a joke, more to me like figments
Of one's imagination, designed to band a structure
Together like the purpose of ligaments.

When it is all said and done, ultimately I get myself in
And then,
I get myself out, like a swimming exhibition.

Or, worst case scenario, I drown.

My glass is almost empty; something must be done about this,
My eyes are bloodshot, speech is slurred,
Nothing is fun about this.

For the thickness of the smoke,
I can barely see the ink I've written on the paper.
Sometimes I cough and I choke.

But this is what I do best, articulate.
What the government defines as law,
I can be relied on to manipulate.

So in a technical perspective, I'm legit.
And I'm not constipated,
But you could say I'm full of shit.

Written by: An Anonymous Alcoholic

U Know Who U Are

Deion Lee III

Selective Fear

I feel like I was judged before you met me. Are there any colors I' ve yet to see? Often I wonder why does the man in the mirror look so strange to me?

When did it all begin, so long ago I don' t remember? Misdirected, tripped, and fell into a bush on a search of love; so in my heart there are many splinters.

Still picking them out today, why must things have gone in such a way?

What could make anyone cross the imaginary line? Some of us have argumentative opinions, and here are some of mine.

I speak of the line imaginary because circumstantial evidence would find that why people seek love in other arms may be of just cause and considered fine.

A conscience can tell one much, and we' ve
all been told to go with our first mind;
however, misunderstanding and lack of
knowledge will lead even the honestly best
intentions blind.

Influence from friends is usually not needed,
for almost everyone who is asked of advice
wants to suggest what they' ve heard,
information repeated.

Clichés, unlike personal, sincere thoughts
are slang about; and those are things we all
can do without.

People decide to engage in relationships
outside of an already existing one… For
what purpose, when, with whom, where,
ultimately WHY?

A relationship, I am emboldened to say, is
healthy with full compromise; and attenuated
by the absence of it, also the creator of lies.

For some will argue that if monogamy doesn' t succeed, then the active participant in the opposite standard must have a suffering condition of greed.

Be that as it may, I agree but also disagree because there is an idea that most won' t feed. Although it' s not morally accepted by most, a void ignored can be grounds to reach out for what you need.

As selfish, nefarious, and certainly disappointing as it sounds, this is a matter necessary of addressing. I am not sure if these words will hinder or help the author or the reader; and if you haven' t happened to notice, I' m confessing.

I believe that I speak on behalf of a significant number of men and women alike; who have made it a primary prerequisite for a lasting relationship to consist of a mandatory display of affection towards one another.

We must be able to visibly see and feel the connection; it doesn' t require a mystical knowledge of zodiac to sense how to react. Each day should continually be a revolving love resurrection.

That is… If it is truly love that you feel. And two wrongs have never been made right. That mentality re-opens a wound, thus taking it longer to heal.

Endurance, strength, and fight reduce when the willingness to cooperate with one another diminishes.

Our generation has grown up under a bad example of what true love is, fact not fiction! Even I assume that I wasn' t taught the proper value and structure of it; on the contrary, I have learned much amidst the malediction.

I observe these old couples, who live together with ailments, along with the battle scars from the troublesome years of their youthful romance; and they can tell you stories that only a lifetime could spawn.

These people overlooked faults, forgave one another without reviving and reliving the memories of the pain, and meant the words FOREVER when they spoke them, to not love in vain.

Contrastingly, we, the young people, have a tendency to act hastily, quickly to resign from commitment, and use our bodies and minds to weariness in a quest of confusion.

Though I may not know much, I am sure that the awareness of legitimate reasons for longevity is part of the solution.

(Truth Is)

Take an active role in your listening skills with your partner. It's crucial. Overall, if and when conflict or problems show up; evaluate what you really want out of life and who you feel the most comfortable living it with. Don' t cheat yourself, because the person you see in the mirror will be reluctant to smile.

Go for what you want and never look back! This is how one should grow old, non-fiction, just a plain fact.

written by: Deion Lee III

A poet by trade, a hobby developed into a talent, later a man out of me was made. And the microphone drops to the floor...

Exposed

I'm most efficacious when taken as directed. It may be in your best interest to follow the instructions written on the labels I have provided for you.

I'm okay on my own, but I'd like to share my life, videlicet with you. I have an idea; however, I don't have a clue.

I left this world a long time ago, picked up my life and took it away from Louisiana. Although here you see my face, the mind behind it is too big for this lil' ole place.

Lord knows I love her. Oh, I love her so! So very much indeed, I had to leave her though.

I can only imagine the pain of a child pantomime, unable to speak, a voice never heard, circumstantially jealous of those who take advantage and the words for granted he or she wishes to someday use.

The tears of an adult derelict are seldom seen, while evidence of sheer misery is found in physical condition and appearance; somehow I became a demigod by society's clearance.

My meals are far from scanty and the fabric of my linens are woven much tighter, yet who would I or anyone else be to assume that my future will be brighter.

I left this world a long time ago, but I don't know where I went, gone somewhere, leaving behind a trail of lament.

On a bustling boulevard, beneath the moon's surveillance, as a doxy makes sheep's eyes at me, a proxy must she be? Is she blue as the azure, and how can I be so sure?

I asked of her to please let me down, for I am too high. She rest her palm on my shoulder as I leaned forth, and in my ear she whispered the reply, "E*ither when I become strong enough to combat my master oppressor or clever enough to foil the plot of his system, bondage will be no more, dreams are desires manifested in mind, noteworthy to hope for. Meanwhile, how may I service you on this night Sir?*"

And down I went, way down, below what anyone could know.

You may have an idea; however, you don't have a clue.

Try to convince yourself that mysteries are mendacious, and then later find them to be true. Who will reinvent the standard of morality and sin next, me or you?

For a book will not substitute experience, as an architect would least likely identify with culinary art.

We can float and swim through waters, thus proving to be impervious to them, correct? But, wait! Are the little things in life insignificant to us?

Even those things that we can't readily see, like the multitude of pores in our flesh that water penetrates.

Not so tough and unabridged after all are we?

Exposed

Written by: Deion Lee III

A Letter To Anesthesia

Dear Anesthesia,

Good day or evening to you. I hope you receive this letter in high spirits and forward progress. I'm fighting for my writes, literary and civil, this life has taken me to an unforeseen height. I've finally found my light!

I'm writing this letter to you because it's the only way I can talk to you before we meet in person. Maybe some who have needed to meet with you have taken similar or more initiative to do as I am doing to gain your correspondence, perhaps not. Nevertheless, this is my cipher, my drawing, and my character.

This impasse of mine will require your hand to help me stand. I ask that before you put me under, to be mindful of my heart, where the problem lies, allow me to re-open my eyes, and make a brand new start.

Thank you for observing this letter, my gratitude is something words cannot begin to express, whether my meeting with you is ineffective versus a success; on either side of the slide I will be relieved of my stress.

Sincerely,

Deion Lee III

P.S. See you soon.

www.ingramcontent.com/pod-product-compliance
Ingram Content Group UK Ltd.
Pitfield, Milton Keynes, MK11 3LW, UK
UKHW020220250726
13967UKWH00001B/103

9 780557 252718